Lessons We Learned from Our Fathers: Reflections from the Men in Our Lives

By David Miller, M.Ed.

Artwork by Ernest Shaw

Cover Layout by Natalie Estelle

Editing by Laurie D. Willis

Dare To Be King Project

Dare To Be King Project
Washington, DC
www.daretobeking.net

Copyright© 2018
ISBN 978-0-692-11044-7

Dare To Be King Project & David Miller

All rights reserved, including the right to reproduce
in whole or in part in any form.

Cover design and layout by Natalie Estelle

Printed in the United States of America.

For the Black men upon whose shoulders I have humbly stood!

When a boy becomes a man

he must change three things in his life:

Playgrounds, Play toys and Playmates

ACKNOWLEDGMENTS

Cross the river in a crowd and the crocodile won't eat you.
~ African proverb

The sad reality is to many folks are so wounded by their relationship with their fathers – or lack thereof – that they can't see the daily transformation occurring in our community.

Every day I'm pleased to see Black fathers pushing strollers and hanging out in the park with their children. I often stop and acknowledge these Black fathers and share a few words of encouragement with them.

Lessons We Learned from Our Fathers is my contribution to promoting the best of Black fatherhood while addressing absentee fathers through quotes from men who have been inspired by their fathers.

Thanks to all of the Black fathers and men who have poured into me, I could fill up numerous pages listing pillars in our community: Peter C. Miller, Sr, Eugene Shelton, Tim Shelton, Sr., Ron Walker, Shawn Dove, Kenneth Braswell, Patrick Paterson, Pastor Linwood Bethea, Elder Dwight Parker, Rev. Dr. Frank Reid, Richard Rowe, Ademola Ekulona, Jerry Craft, Mark Booker, Darryl Green, Paul Coates (Black Classic Press), Brother Nati (Everyone's Place), Olamina Stevenson, Joel Austin, Andre Turner & Matt Stevens.

Special thanks to Dr. Lawrence Jackson, a childhood friend, great dad and one of the foremost biographers in the country focused on shaping narratives about Black people for helping me understand the importance of documenting our stories.

To my cultural fathers who shaped my thinking: John Henrik Clarke, Malcolm X, Paul Robeson, Kwame Nkrumah, Muhammad Ali, Haki Mahubuti and Randall Robinson.

Much gratitude extended to Bro. Ernest Shaw from Baltimore for his amazing artistic contribution, Natalie Estelle for book cover layout and Laurie Willis for editorial contributions.

My work would not be possible without my loving and supportive family. To my wife Karla and my children, Kelsye, Jihad & Mikalei, who help me understand each day the power of a committed father in the lives of his children, thank you for helping me stay grounded and focused on what's really important.

Finally, to my parents Peter & Carol Miller (R.I.P. mom), who guided me all my life with the perfect amounts of nurturing, discipline and love; I owe you more than I could ever repay. Additionally, special thanks to my father for providing me with a solid blueprint for fatherhood.

DEDICATION

Riots are the language of the unheard

~Dr. Martin Luther King

Growing up I was blessed with a father who is larger than life. I was raised in West Baltimore, and my father has always been my hero. Being raised and surrounded by strong Black men all my life created a clear sense of responsibility in me and armed me with the necessary weaponry to confront racism.

Likewise, the strong Black men in my life taught me how to navigate Baltimore's mean streets while simultaneously helping me understand important principles like educational attainment, hard work, empathy and giving back.

Lessons We Learned from Our Fathers is dedicated to my father, Peter C. Miller, Sr., and all of the nameless, faceless, seldom recognized and often-marginalized Black fathers who raise children daily in a toxic society.

This book honors all of the brothers you never hear about on the news who are actively engaged fathers. They're not committing crimes or disturbing the peace so they receive zero coverage. Yet, we've all seen young brothers pushing strollers in the hood or feeding their young warriors or princesses on the subway. We've seen them because they exist. Society may not want to acknowledge them, but we all know they exist.

It appears an increasing number of Black fathers across the country are "woke," meaning they're fully engaged in raising children to be scholars, community transformational leaders, spiritual anchors and individuals who love and care about humanity.

While we may never see their names or photographs in The Washington Post or The New York Times, these men have created a standard in their homes and within their families by modeling Black manhood in its truest form.

It's seldom acknowledged or discussed, the Black community has a rich legacy of fathers who have blazed trails, uplifted families and maintained the richness of family and community life.

Whether we look at larger-than-life fathers like Muhammad Ali, Malcolm X, Paul Robeson and Martin Luther King, Jr. or ordinary, resilient fathers, there are millions of Black men who are all committed to the virtues of authentic fatherhood.

From Travis, a teen father I met on the train in Newark, New Jersey, to Charles, fifty-seven, a father with children ages thirty-seven, eighteen and four, who I met while facilitating Breakfast with Dads in East Baltimore, Black fathers are handling their responsibilities. Many fathers are working multiple jobs and also caring for non-biological children they "inherited" with blended families.

For Craig, another father I met, the demands of being a relatively young father with multiple children have become overwhelming. Craig spent five years in prison and is engaged to Tina, a hospital receptionist. Craig and Tina both have two children and are raising four children as a blended family.

Craig works at hotel by day and stocks shelves part-time at night. He's hard working and, based on our conversation, I gather he's a loving and committed father who recently gained custody of his two sons.

These shining examples of Black fatherhood – and countless others – provide ample opportunities to rewrite narratives about fatherhood in the Black community.

Lessons We Learned from Our Fathers is a manifesto dedicated to Black fathers far and near who remain committed to their families and their communities.

Throughout this book, you will read terms like exceptional, authentic and heroic. These terms are used describe the Black fathers I know personally and meet regularly during my travels.

Unfortunately, an increasing number of Black children are being raised without spending time with sober, responsible, spiritually guided fathers or father figures. The charge for us who fit this description is to reach back into our communities and mentor, support, talk to and spend time with these young people who lack fathers in their lives.

It is my sincere hope that this book elevates the conversation about Black fathers as assets versus deficits. It is clear to me that re-imaging Black fathers as an essential part of life and community development can position the Black community to seriously addresses the urban street violence, HIV/AIDS, poverty and apathy that plague many Black communities.

RE-IMAGING BLACK FATHERS

By David Miller

See Black fathers praying with their children

See Black fathers changing diapers

See Black fathers walking through the hood strolling young princes in strollers

See Black fathers braiding hair or fixing their daughter's ponytail

See Black fathers at PTA meetings

See Black fathers helping with homework

See Black fathers honoring Black mothers

See Black fathers frying catfish and steaming collard greens

See Black fathers at the barbershop directing their son's first haircut

See Black fathers reading bedtime stories

See Black fathers walking their daughters down the aisle

If you look closely, these are things Black fathers do daily!

INTRODUCTION

Lessons We Learned from Our Fathers serves as 'cliff notes' for busy dads balancing their professional and personal lives. The book is also designed to inspire dads who are serious about improving their relationships with their children.

This book provides motivation, strength and encouragement for all the days you feel like giving up, for the days you feel overwhelmed or the days your children make bad decisions and you take it personally. Likewise, it's a great tool for the days when Black fathers and the mothers of their children are not on the same page and/or reading from the same book.

The book is designed to inspire Black fathers to keep pushing and never give up no matter how difficult their fatherhood journey gets. Black fathers should glean nuggets of wisdom from the book to strengthen their connectedness with their children.

To write Lessons We Learned from Our Fathers, I interviewed hundreds of Black fathers across the county, soliciting quotes and advice from fathers, grandfathers, uncles, coaches, barbers and others who have stood in the gap providing men with fatherly advice. Many of these men were haunted by their own traumatic relationships with their fathers, yet they were able to draw wisdom from "village dads" and elders within the greater community who help guide their fatherhood journey.

While many reports and documentaries focus on the "war stories" of Black fatherhood, we thought it prudent to highlight the awesome relationship between Black fathers and their children.

Additionally, I felt it essential to demystify Black fathers and provide accurate information about us. Over the last ten years, several important milestones and anecdotes have crystalized the conversation about Black fathers.

On January twentieth, two thousand and nine, the world witnessed the inauguration of the first person of African descent to be elected President of the United States. A young, charismatic, married father of two moved in to Sixteen Hundred Pennsylvania Ave. President Barack Hussein Obama, a Harvard-educated man, assumed the role of the commander and chief.

While the nation was transfixed on the Obama family, anticipating subsequent policy changes to improve the economy, increase jobs, make difficult foreign policy decisions and address corporate greed, families in the Black community were excited to see an educated, polished Black father in the driver's seat.

President Obama candidly talked about his own struggles over being raised by a single mom and the emotional challenges his father's absence created. His acknowledgement of the problems he faced while navigating society without a father, just as do so many other Black and Brown boys and girls, was refreshing.

In two thousand and thirteen after the shooting death of Trayvon Martin, President Obama delivered an eloquent yet emotional speech that underscored his compassion for Black youth. While his remarks created a media firestorm, "Trayvon Martin could have been me thirty-five years ago" was an important stand taken by a Black father regardless of his celebrity status.

The second major milestone over the last decade was a report released by The Centers for Disease Control and Prevention's National Center for Health Statistics that provided an important spin on the notion of Black fathers as deadbeat or dead broke dads.

While most realize the absence of fathers in the Black community is still a persistent challenge, the report indicated that Black fathers were statistically more involved in their children's lives than fathers of other racial groups were.

These two major anecdotes represent a renewed sense of hope for Black fathers and families. While so much work is still needed, an acknowledgement of our humanity coupled with the deconstruction of popular myths about Black fathers has been monumental.

Stroll through most American cities and you'll notice an interesting phenomenon: young fathers picking up their children from school or walking them in a stroller.

While this is not new, I have begun noticing more and more fathers of all ages hanging out with their children. From Oakland, California, to Jackson, Mississippi, I chronicled these encounters and conversations with fathers in front of places as specific as the Jamaican carryout to sites as common place as Walgreens.

The emergence of Black men publicly parenting their children and the outstanding way I was reared by my mother AND father, motivated me to republish a book I wrote in 2002, "Lessons I Learned from My Father.

"Lessons We Learned from Our Fathers" is a masterful collection of thought-provoking essays, personal reflections and quotes from ordinary Black fathers.

It is our hope that this book will be dissected and internalized by fathers young and old as a tool to spark courageous conversations about fatherhood in the Black community.

TABLE OF CONTENTS

CHAPTER ONE
Authentic Fatherhood
19

CHAPTER TWO
Personification of Black Fathers on TV
25

CHAPTER THREE
Optimal Mental Health
32

CHAPTER FOUR
Family Life and Community Development
51

CHAPTER FIVE
Father as a God Force
69

CHAPTER SIX
Building Legacy
74

Fathers are the secret weapon in the community!

Before Reading…

Thought-provoking questions are inquiries that shine light on the essence of lives and force us to think about hopes, dreams and aspirations.

The best way to get to know you is by asking yourself the right questions. People who continually ask themselves questions that provoke introspection will, in effect, create a foundation for happier lives that are rich with purpose and meaning.

"Lessons We Learned from Our Fathers" tells the stories of fathers who are empowering their families and shaping the lives of their children.

I gave fathers a specific set of questions to internalize before writing the book questions that should spark honest conversation about their fatherhood journeys. For those of you blessed to have a good father with whom you're in contact, I encourage you to interview him about his life and record the conversation for posterity

Sadly, many of the fathers we interviewed never took advantage of the opportunity to connect on a deeper level with their fathers. Instead, most shared regrets about not taking advantage of the time they spent with their fathers.

The questions I pose are based on reflections I gleaned from interviews with Black fathers, grandfathers, village dads and other male figures. I have been blessed to talk with my dad about many of these questions, and I had my son interview my father, who he calls Pop Pop.

Each question explores the daily thoughts of Black fathers and places special emphasis on the contemporary issues challenging most fathers today. I'm sure you're wondering how I narrowed it down to only forty questions when there are hundreds of valid questions that could have been asked.

I hope many of you will use these questions to assess your fatherhood journey or, more importantly, to reconnect with your purpose as fathers.

I encourage you to take some time reflecting on each question. Read them all carefully and give yourself permission to be vulnerable when answering them.

1. When did you realize you were becoming a man? Explain.

2. What was the hardest thing you went through as a child and how did you overcome it?

3. Did your father talk to you about race or racism? Explain.

4. What was your relationship with your father like?

5. What kind of relationship did you have with your grandfather? (When answering, please specify whether it was your paternal grandfather (dad's father) or your maternal grandfather (mom's father).

6. What qualities do you most respect in a woman?

7. What does authentic fatherhood look like?

8. How can Black fathers better support the mothers of their children?

9. What are the three biggest events that most shaped your life?

10. How do we reclaim the sacred essence of fatherhood?

11. How do we change the negative image and perceptions of Black fathers?

12. What can society to do reengage Black fathers and reconnect them with their children?

13. Who were some of the other men in your life that helped shape your temperament as a father?

14. Where would you rank spirituality in your fatherhood journey? Explain.

15. Have you considered therapy? Have you struggled with depression and/or other mental health challenges?
16. What would you characterize as your greatest success during your fatherhood journey?
17. What do you love most about being a father?
18. What do you remember about when your child (ren) were born?
19. How important has communication (being able to listen) been throughout your fatherhood journey?
20. What do you give your children that you didn't get from your father (virtues, emotions skills etc.)? Explain.
21. What three adjectives would your grandfather use to describe you?
22. Is there anything you wish you had told your children?
23. What has been your biggest regret during your fatherhood journey?
24. If you had it to do over, what's the one thing you would have done differently as a father?
25. What are you most proud of in life?
26. What kind of legacy are you building for your family?
27. What three words would you say best describe who you tried to be in life and how you want to be remembered?
28. What is the toughest decision you have made as a father?
29. Do you think it's easier or harder to be a father now than when you were a child?
30. Is there anything you regret not having asked your parents?
31. Do you think today's fathers have it harder or easier than fathers from past generations?

32. Were you ever scared to be a parent? Explain.

33. What's the best or most important thing your father can do for you right now?

34. Have other male figures and/or village dads helped to raise you?

35. In what ways are your children like you? Explain.

36. What makes you lose your temper with your children?

37. What are the three best decisions you've made as a father?

38. What traditions did your father pass on to you that you passed on to your children?

39. What can you do to inspire and motivate other Black fathers?

40. What are you most thankful for as a father?

CHAPTER ONE
Authentic Fatherhood

Moving toward a new definition of fatherhood
and creating daily living standard

But stay woke!
Childish Gambino

Authentic Black Fatherhood

It is hard to find words to describe the essence of a father. A father is the spiritual and moral compass of his family. He's an emotional provider, protector, disciplinarian, friend and confidant. A father is a loving human being who sacrifices daily to ensure the needs of his family and children are met. A father places his own material needs to the side for the betterment of his family. A father realizes his job, although hard, if done right produces major dividends for his family, children and future grandchildren. A father detests acts of violence, corruption and criminal acts that handicap his community. Authentic fatherhood requires men to always put family and the God of their understanding first and to honor the following pillars:

First Teacher and Disciplinarian

Being a father means you are your child's first teacher. In addition, one of the most important roles you perform as a father is teaching your child about society's written and unwritten rules, and helping him or her understand the power of decision-making and accepting responsibilities for his or her own actions.

As your child grows up, he or she will face many distractions from technology to friends. Fathers teach their children about limits, boundaries and discipline. They also help their children form values about life while grasping the importance of education as an essential tool for growth and upward mobility. Perhaps Nelson Mandela, the late, great South African president and humanitarian said it best: "Education is the most powerful weapon which you can use to change the world."

Safety and Security

When a man receives the news that he is becoming a father, whether or not the pregnancy is planned, whether or not he and the woman carrying his child are a couple and even if he's not happy about the news, it is his responsibility to begin creating a safe, secure and nurturing environment for his child.

Spending Quality Time

Knowing how to balance work and family time is key for authentic fathers. While I understand a man must provide financially for his family, I also know there are a lot of fathers who allow their career to cause them to miss school plays, Parent-Teacher conferences and extra-curricular activities in which their children are participating. I understand the desire to make money and get job promotions, but at the end of the day, missed school functions and ball games are one-time only deals and cannot be repeated or "made up for."

Fathers should ensure they create in their schedules fun activities with their kids, including exercising, playing games, going to movies and attending their extra-curricular events like sporting events and orchestra and band concerts. Making time to talk and listen to your children makes a big difference. We are living during a unique time, and our children have unprecedented access to information and technology that can be very distracting. In many respects, sadly talking has become a lost art between many fathers and their children.

> The best advice I received from my father (Phillip Banks). Whatever you do in life, always make decisions that don't jeopardize your integrity. Your integrity isn't for sale. Without it, you have nothing.
>
> David Banks,
> New York, New York

Unconditional Love

From the day your child leaves the hospital to come home, your patience will be tested. As they grow up, your children will make mistakes. However, no matter what they do or say, being a father or mother means you will love your children unconditionally.

Research suggests children who receive love and attention from their fathers are less likely to drop out of school, use drugs and become involved in criminal behavior.

> " It's my job to give you as many chances to succeed in life as possible. R.I. P., Dad (Darryl Unseld, Sr.)
>
> Darryl Unseld, Jr (Louisville, Kentucky) "

Hug and kiss your children daily and show them love. Listen intently as your child shares daily activities and school experiences.

In today's society, which is chock full of reality shows and movies that often depict Black fathers as reckless and irresponsible, it is critically important to always reflect on the contributions of fathers and the countless men who step up to serve as fathers for children whose fathers aren't in their lives. These men are often stepfathers, coaches, pastors, barbers and other men who assume the awesome responsibilities of helping children define their lives.

For this, we say thank you

To the biological fathers who don't give up on your children even when times get difficult or even when you and your child's mom don't see eye to eye on anything, thank you for teaching me how to navigate the world, spot danger and act accordingly.

To the stepfathers, a term I've never liked, incidentally, thank you for stepping into the gaps, for being solid role models and for loving your wives' children unconditionally.

To the village dads, a group of men you find in every community, who recognize the need to support and provide love and guidance to children and youth, thank you for doing what you do and for being there. Often, "village dads" are young people whose fathers may or may not be active in their lives. These heroes appear in our communities in many forms, including as teachers, coaches, neighbors and others, and they all fill a huge void.

> " My father was my first teacher. As I got older, he reminded me that your children's success depends on your ability to teach them how to navigate life. These powerful words have helped me raise five sons who all graduated from college.
>
> Albert C. Smalls (Brooklyn, New York) "

As the sun rises and falls…so will you through life… but remember the sun always comes back! I heard my grandfather say this all the time but didn't really understand until I got older.

Robert Parrish
(Prince Georges County, MD)

For most of my life, I hated my father. Things didn't work out between he and my mom, and I was consumed by anger. My grandfather helped me understand the power of unconditional love. I learned some powerful life lessons from my grandfather.

Edgar Rivera
(Queens, New York)

"

Going to the library with my dad was always a ritual growing up. As a father of two, I have continued the ritual of taking my children to the library on Saturday's. This is one way we spend quality time together.

Franklin Marshall
(Chester, Pennsylvania)

CHAPTER TWO
The Personification of Black fathers on TV

f they don't know your dreams,
then they can't shoot 'em down.
Rapper J. Cole

The Personification of Black Fathers on TV

I always remind myself how blessed I am to have grown up with my father and to have had relationships with both of my grandfathers, Eugene Shelton and Warnie Miller. My grandfathers are two exceptional Black men who, though Jim Crow affected them, provided for their families physically and psychologically. Shelton and Miller were able to adapt to an extreme brand of racial segregation seldom discussed in the north and instill an overarching sense of spiritual and moral excellence in their children.

Additionally, I benefited from having what I called cultural fathers, who I could view at home on the TV set. Two that always rise to the top are James Evans, the hardworking, loving father on "Good Times," and Bill Cosby, who portrayed a doctor on "The Cosby Show." On the set, Cosby was married to a lawyer with whom he had five wonderful children, and he often wore T-shirts or sweaters that gave props to Historically Black Colleges and Universities. Evans and Cosby were undoubtedly the most impactful Black TV dads in my world.

James Evans and his wife Florida raised their family at 921 North Gilbert Avenue, apartment 17C in Chicago's Cabrini-Green projects. Cabrini-Green was considered one of the most dangerous public housing sites in America. "Good Times" provided America with a glimpse of the daily struggles of Black families by navigating sensitive topics like heroin addiction, food deserts, gang violence, white privilege and substandard living conditions.

James exercised tough love to prepare his children, J.J., Thelma and Michael, for Southside Chicago's mean streets. John Amos played James on the sitcom; Esther Rolle played Florida.

"Good Times" debuted on February 8, 1974, and ended on August 1, 1979. Over the years, several networks have featured reruns of the show, which had a subtext that centered on James, the family patriarch and a Korean War veteran who struggles to maintain a decent-paying job. A hard-working, proud Black father, James was forced to bounce from job to job based on a variety of factors. He struggled to earn a living wage based on his lack of a formal education and Chicago's dysfunctional labor market. Weekly viewers got to witness James and Florida pay rent, put food on the table and raise three gregarious children.

"The Cosby Show" featured Bill Cosby as Dr. Heathcliff "Cliff" Huxtable, a fun-loving dad with an amazing relationship with his five children, Sondra, Denise, Theo, Vanessa and Rudy. The show was set in Brooklyn Heights, New York, with Cliff and his wife, portrayed by co-star Phylicia Rashad, who were highly skilled professionals -- Cliff an obstetrician and Clair a well-established attorney.

Black fathers set a standard in the 1980s and 1990s on network TV. "Uncle Phil" Banks (James Avery), one of the main characters on The Fresh Prince of Bel-Air, demonstrated true fatherhood by providing a home for his children, Hilary, Carlton, Ashley and Nicholas, openly displaying love for them and disciplining them when necessary. He also treated his wife's nephew, Will, a street-wise teen from the inner city of Philadelphia (Will Smith), as he treated his biological children. One of the most touching scenes in the show's six-year history – in fact, one of the most touching scenes in TV period – occurred in the episode when Will's truck driver father (Ben Vereen), reneged on his promise to let Will spend the summer traveling the country with him. After denouncing his father and saying he'd grow up to be just fine without him, Will broke down in tears and asked, "Why don't he want me, man?" as "Uncle Phil" grabbed him and they embraced as the camera panned to a figurine of a father holding his son that Will had purchased as a gift for his father.

Other Black TV fathers like Lester Jenkins on "227," George Jefferson on "The Jeffersons," Carl Winslow on "Family Matters," Fred Sanford on "Sanford and Son," "Rock," Charles Dutton, a

> "When we were children, my dad made us watch "The Cosby Show." As I got older, I understood why my father insisted we watch a show with a strong Black male character as a responsible father – something my father didn't experience growing up.
>
> Today I still watch reruns of the show with my daughter.
>
> Harold Windsor
> (Douglasville, Georgia)

hardworking dad in Baltimore, Julius Rock on "Everybody Hates Chris," Michael Kyle on "My Wife and Kids" and Bernie Mac on "The Bernie Mac Show" helped to shape America's understanding of the role of Black fathers over the last two decades.

As a high school student, I used to rush home from wrestling practice, complete my chores, eat dinner and be ready to watch "The Cosby Show" with my parents. NBC's "The Cosby Show" originally aired on September 20, 1984, and ran until April 30, 1992.

From Theo's learning disability to Denise's challenges staying focused on college and career opportunities, "The Cosby Show" challenged stereotypes about Black families.

Over the past decade or so, my children have come to enjoy watching "The Cosby Show" and the relationship between Cliff Huxtable (Bill Cosby) and his children.

> My dad always made time for us growing up. He worked a blue-collar job and came home most nights beaten up from his hard work. Years later, many nights I came home exhausted just like my dad, but I still tried to watch "The Bernie Mac Show" with my kids. I'm sure most nights I fell asleep on it, but spending time with my children has always been priceless.
>
> Marty Johnson (Flint, Michigan)

"Good Times" and "The Cosby Show" were important examples of the breadth and depth of responsible fatherhood. Both sitcoms shaped an entire generation, providing realistic examples of Black fathers as life giving and life sustaining parts of their family and community.

Unfortunately, Bill Cosby was found guilty of sexual assault in 2018, after years of sexual assault allegations levied against him by dozens of women. Even before Cosby's trial and subsequent conviction, many networks had discontinued "The Cosby Show" reruns, some universities stripped Cosby of the honorary degrees they'd bestowed upon him and Spelman College in Atlanta terminated a professorship endowed by Cosby and his wife Camille – all of which exacerbated the already severely tarnished reputation of the one-time beloved dad who changed the narrative about Black fathers on TV.

In September 2017, "Blackish" debuted as an innovative modern version of "The Cosby Show." It stars Anthony Anderson and Tracee Ellis Ross. Anderson plays Andre "Dre" Johnson, Sr., an advertising executive who's a graduate of historic Howard University in Washington, D.C.

Ross plays Dr. Rainbow Johnson, an anesthesiologist and graduate of Brown University. The show features a Black family living on the West Coast dealing with a plethora of issues including the election of Donald Trump, racism, police brutality and the use of the N-Word.

On the show, Dre and Rainbow are raising four smart, creative children. Other prominent characters are Dre's divorced parents, played by Academy Award

> "As a little boy, I used to love going to my grandparents' house, where I would watch "Sanford and Son" with Pop Pop. The interaction between father and son (Fred and Lamont) on the show was priceless.
>
> I hope to live long enough to do the same thing with my grandkids."
>
> Mike Miller
> (Newark, New Jersey)

nominee and veteran actor Laurence J. Fishburne, III, and Emmy nominated actress Jenifer Lewis.

"Black-ish" is another shining example of authentic Black fatherhood on screen and shares with audiences the highs and lows of balancing home life and work.

Over the past four decades, millions of Black families have benefitted from the essence of resilient Black fathers on TV. From the 1972 debut episode of "Sanford and Son" to "Black-ish," the Black community has a repository of healthy images of Black fathers that can be viewed regularly on a variety of networks.

> Uncle Phil (James Avery) on "The Fresh Prince of Bel-Air" reminded me of my stepfather. Uncle Phil was larger than life and accepted Will into the family with open arms. Although this was a TV show, that bond between Uncle Phil and Will left a lasting impression on me.
>
> Glen Wilson
> (Boston, Massachusetts)

❝ I watch "Black-ish" with my children because it reminds me of watching "The Cosby Show" back in the day with my dad.

It's great to see strong images of Black fathers on television! ❞

Bobby Blake (New Haven, Connecticut)

❝ Andre "Dre" Johnson on the show "Black-ish" reminds me of my father.

I love watching the show with my two daughters because it's a constant reminder to America that strong Black fathers are omnipresent. ❞

Rodney Isaac (Buffalo, New York)

CHAPTER THREE
Optimal Mental Health

Tell me how I stay positive
When they never see good in me?

Kendrick Lamar

Optimal Mental Health

"In a moment of crisis, the wise build bridges and the foolish build dams"

~ Nigerian proverb~

Several months ago, I posted an image and caption about mental health on Facebook and Twitter. To my surprise, I received sixty-seven inbox messages thanking me for the post and inquiring about therapy. While I am not a clinician, I have always had a unique talent for getting Black men to open up about sensitive issues. I guess this may, in part, be due to the fact that many of my friends and my wife are clinicians serving a variety of populations.

Several of the posts were from men we would consider well-to-do, Black men who always seem together. They dress in Brooks Brothers suits, expensive, wing-tipped Ferragamo shoes and French cuff shirts. They work in corporate America and have law degrees from Yale or other Ivy League schools and push Jaguars, BMWs or other luxury vehicles like Mercedes Benz.

By contrast, some of the posts were from ordinary guys struggling to come to grips with their own mental health issues and the challenges they now face that result from childhood traumas and setbacks they've endured as adults.

These men were reaching out to me to talk about dark places, childhood trauma, coping with racism and a plethora of issues all associated with mental health.

All of the men were fathers, with children ranging toddlers to adults. Each shared in his own way a feeling of being incomplete and/or struggling with the concept of fatherhood.

Divorce, child support payments, visitation and being the offspring of unwed parents were commonalities linking this group of men though they were from different cities and had never met.

We discussed what I call the big four, challenges that impact Black fathers moving toward optimal mental health:

- Stigma-- a fixed attitude suggesting that Black men who seek treatment are weak or societal failures.

- Treatment-- ongoing challenges finding Black male therapists and/or culturally competent therapists who understand the impact of racism and white supremacy on Black men.

- Access/Insurance-- while a barrier in most cities, numerous organizations provide mental health services on a sliding-fee schedule. While paying out of pocket may be a challenge, if our own mental health is a priority we may have to live on a budget and determine ways to afford bi-weekly therapy sessions.

The discussion was intimate, provocative and real. The topic of suicide usually came up at some point, along with addictions to sex, porn, gambling, drugs and alcohol.

Overwhelmingly, the men ranged from young brothers in their early twenties to elderly brothers in their sixties.

Consistently, the conversations involved traumatic experiences, dealing with parental absences and early exposure to violence. Some even discussed physical and sexual abuse at the hands of their father or other trusted male relatives.

Most of the men just wanted to share as a precursor to being connected to a Black male therapist, or at the very least, a Black female therapist who understands Black masculinity.

> Being a father to my kids has been the most rewarding experience of my life. Even when things got tough as an unmarried "Black man" raising two boys, I did not give up!

Jim Thompson
(Winston Salem, North Carolina)

I connected with several of the brothers over coffee, though I usually ordered Green Tea when we met.

These conversations helped me understand my own trauma associated with exposure to violence in my late adolescence and my own experiences with the court system as I fought to see my daughter.

The true mark of courage is to take care of your family, by any means necessary!

Craig Smalls
(Portland, Oregon)

I was able to directly connect many of the brothers with therapists in several cities across the country.

The experience was both eye opening and cathartic and pushed me to think about ways I can support Black men in the realm of mental health. Questions dance through my mind about ways to address the stigma surrounding mental health while at the same time honoring the strength of Black men.

The challenges of always being on "Alert," preoccupied with your own mortality and figuring out ways to keep your family together and safe are overwhelming. Confronting racism, Jim Crow, James Crow and navigating potentially dangerous encounters with the police,

Coupled with the pressures of being a good, consistent father have rendered many Black men emotionally bankrupt.

To this end, it is critically important for the sake of our families that we seek culturally competent therapists to assist us with navigating the challenges that prevent optimum mental health. Additionally, we have identified several key items that we believe help Black fathers focus on the power of mental health and wellness.

Courage

Fathering and responsible parenting are at minimum a twenty-five-year commitment. With all of the distractions in society today, fathers are needed now more than ever to set high standard in households.

Much of the research tells us that being a good father helps foster empathy, honesty, self-reliance, self-control, kindness and cooperation. It also promotes intellectual curiosity, motivation and a desire to achieve. It helps protect children from developing anxiety, depression, eating disorders and anti-social behavior and from abusing alcohol and drugs.

Being a responsible father takes courage and the willingness to deal with difficult the landscape often confronted by Black fathers. Fatherhood is a huge responsibility, and many of the fathers we interviewed felt that if their child isn't doing well academically and socially they have failed.

> When you were born, I wanted to walk away,
>
> but I realized you needed me to grow up to be a strong man.
>
> These were powerful words coming from my father.
>
> Wayne Johnson-Bey
> (Washington, D.C.)

A few helpful tips:

> I have successfully raised three sons. My sons have never been arrested, each graduated from high school and not one fathered a child until he was at least twenty-one years of age.
>
> When asked what I did, I always reply: I didn't give up on my sons.
>
> Malcolm Anthony Wilson (Chicago, Illinois)

1. Create Family Rituals—It's important for fathers to create family rituals to help guide their children at an early age. For example, a father could establish a household rule that his children cannot watch TV between four p.m. and seven p.m., time that is reserved for doing homework and reading books for leisure to gain knowledge.

2. Let Your Children Earn Independence -- While it's important to set limits for your children to give them a sense of self-control, you should also encourage their independence to make choices within those limits.

3. Be Flexible -- Children grow up quickly, so be sure to keep up with their development. In other words, know your child.

Courage is the ability for men to deal with obstacles that life presents. Courage is never leaving your family, even when times are tough.

John Templeton
(Boston, Massachusetts)

I realized how courageous my father was when I realized he had only a fifth-grade education but he put three of us through college.

Carlos Rogers
(Seattle, Washington)

I learned valuable lessons from my father and grandfather about courage and commitment. Courage was defined in my house by a man's ability to respond to the needs of the family – whether they were physical, financial or spiritual ...

Ed McMichael
(Mobile, Alabama)

Courage is one of the major characteristics that distinguish a good father from an exceptional father.

Ruben Thompson
(Augusta, Georgia)

My basketball coach was the only father I had growing up. He would always insist that we have the courage to be honest about our shortcomings.

Ron Allen Thomas
(Buffalo, New York)

Coping with Racism

To say racism is alive and well is an understatement. I remember just getting back to the Airbnb house I rented from a long day volunteering at school in a suburb of Accra, Ghana. The day was August thirteenth, and as I turned on my laptop, CNN was airing footage of a mob of white protesters rioting in Charlottesville, VA.

The white supremacists were armed with sticks, bottles and other projectiles, and the world watched the ugliness of it all in full affect. When the smoke cleared, several innocent protesters had been injured and Heather Heyer, a thirty-two-year-old paralegal, had been struck by a car and killed during the riot.

Some fifty-four years since passage of the historic Civil Rights Act of 1964, which was followed a year later by the historic Voting Rights Act, America still grapples with the issue of race every day.

In my opinion, racism is one of the most complex social issues impacting the Western world. The arrests of Rashon Nelson and Donte Robinson, two Black men who were arrested in a Philadelphia Starbucks while waiting for a third person to start a business meeting, went viral. Moreover, their arrest is among other similar incidents of police brutality that have gone viral on social media.

Many would agree that we live in a society that is still "separate but unequal." One of the questions on the hearts and minds of many parents is how do we talk to our children about race, racism, bias and bigotry.

> " My biggest fear is that I have not taught my son enough to deal with racism and bigotry in a society rife with both. "
>
> Jason Applegate (Cincinnati, Ohio)

> " Next to sex, conversations about race/racism are the fundamental things that I talk with my sons about. We cannot let our children experience racism on their own. "
>
> Max Bailey-EL (Philadelphia, Pennsylvania)

Recently during a session with fathers, several men in the Daddy Meet Up Group raised the question. Each voiced concerns and frustrations about educating his children and the dangers of racism.

As the conversation grew more heated, it become acutely apparent that fathers have a moral, ethical and spiritual obligation to teach their children to have the confidence to confront racism and stand up for themselves.

" Who will teach our boys about racism if we are not present?

Strong men involved in family and community life help to neutralize racism and white supremacy. "

Terry Prince
(Queens, New York)

White men will never respect Black men if Black men do not respect themselves, their women, their children and their communities!

Craig Rivera
(Waterloo, Iowa)

"Never discuss these three things with white folks: Race, Religion or Politics".

Michael Campbell
(Rochester, NY)

If I am unable to teach my teenage son anything else, I must train him to be able to live in a country that despises him.

Rod Wills, Sr.
(Atlanta, Georgia)

"Never accept discrimination or abuse … Also work on behalf of the oppressed."

Derrick Harvey
(Washington, D.C.)

We live in a country where a white police officer can shoot and kill an unarmed Black man on camera and get away with it.

Calvin Winters
(Oklahoma City, Oklahoma)

My grandfather told us to always maintain a healthy suspicion of white folks.

Ray Quick (Newark, New Jersey)

Anger

In 1968, two noted Black psychiatrists, William H. Grier and Price M. Cobbs, released the groundbreaking book, "Black Rage," which looked deeply into the sources of anger within the Black community.

The issues of anger and rage among Black men remain timely and important topics. As often discussed in several of the fatherhood groups I facilitated over the years, anger is a normal, natural emotion that can often lead to self-destructive behaviors.

In the spectrum of emotions, anger seems to be one of the most accepted among men. Anger has become one of the major challenges that men must confront to maintain healthy/productive lives. Fathers and men must train their children in the "art" of self-control and tactical anger. The regulation of self-control helps to ensure that anger does not become a debilitating factor in the lives of youth.

> Many say anger is the only emotion that Black men show. I taught my sons that anger is a natural emotion that must be controlled. I taught my sons how to be "tactically angry." Anger is not always a bad thing.
>
> Jahid Turner
> (Nashville, Tennessee)

As a direct result of anger, we have lost thousands of Black men to prison, substance abuse and early death (stress and homicides). Although anger is a natural human emotion, teaching boys effective ways to manage anger will reduce community violence and improve conditions within communities.

> Fathers must teach their sons about anger and the consequences of allowing anger to control how they deal with conflicts.
> Tavor Singleton (Trenton, New Jersey)

Fathers must be in place to help their children confront the anger that exists as a direct result of racism and oppression. Through modeling appropriate techniques to manage anger, fathers play a huge role in helping boys understand the power of resolving conflicts!

In many instances, children look toward their fathers to help them understand how to deal with challenging situations. While mothers play an important role as well, seeing men deal with conflicts is developmentally important for children.

When fathers are not present, children and youth are often trained by external factors and use violence to deal with situations or people that make them angry.

Even in my own life I can recount the times when my failure to manage my anger has caused potentially dire circumstances.

While often minimized in society, a healthy father/child relationship can help address issues related to anger and frustration.

> I used to get so angry that I would hit my girlfriend in front of our son. I never realized he would grow up to think it was okay to hit women. My son is now seventeen, and he beats his girlfriend. I blame myself. I have some work to do with my son.
>
> Juan Jones (Bronx, New York)

> My father taught us early that anger causes so many Black men to go to prison. The best advice he gave us is to realize what makes you angry and deal with it – without violence.
>
> J.T. Lee (Phoenix, Arizona)

> Every man in my family has been to prison. I just recently came home after serving six years. I had to go to prison to learn how to control my anger... I must make sure my son learns the power of anger. I cannot allow what has happened to me and the men in my family to happen to my son.
>
> Akil Houston (Cincinnati, Ohio)

> Anger and rage have devastated my family. Almost all of the men in my family have gone to prison for some reason or another. Yoga has helped me break the cycle in the Williams family. My grandfather always warned me about the anger issue that all of the men in my family have.
>
> Teddy Bilal Williams (Grand Rapid, Michigan)

> My daughters are angry because of divorce and separation. My mom and dad got divorced when I was in high school. The anger my daughters exhibit is the same kind of anger I dealt with as a teenager. I talk to my father daily about being a better man and father to my daughters.
>
> C.J. Brown (Seattle, Washington)

Helping my daughter manage and control her anger is a matter of life and death.

We live in Detroit and so many young girls are getting arrested because of fights in school and in the community.

My father has helped me understand how much my daughter needs me to be a shining example of Black manhood.

Thomas Mann
(Detroit, Michigan)

Depression

Several years ago, during a heated discussion among a group of Black men about child support and child custody, one of the brothers started crying and shaking uncontrollably.

I immediately decided to take a ten-minute break. Several fathers went to the parking lot to smoke cigarettes, and a few others checked their text messages.

A few minutes passed, and the brother continued sobbing in his seat. I was amazed that none of the other dads in the group engaged this young brother.

After a brief chat with him, I realized just how real depression and stress are in the lives of Black men. He talked to me about his ongoing custody battle and several other traumatic incidents that had unfolded in his life over the past few months.

Our group ended around 8:30 p.m., and most of the other dads gathered their belongings and left. I hung around to share a few resources with the brother to help him navigate the multiple systems, which were dramatically impacting his life.

The conversation reminded me of a book I was given by a colleague that I'd started reading earlier in the week, "Black Men and Depression: Understanding and Overcoming Depression in Black Men." The work chronicled John Head's twenty-five-year battle with depression. Head, like so many Black men, worked every day but masked his depression-related pain.

Several weeks passed and I noticed the brother was missing from the group. I reached out to him to check on his progress and was pleased to hear he was involved in individual therapy to address his ongoing issues with depression. He shared that because of therapy and some support from Legal Aid; he has a better outlook on life and has established communication with his estranged children.

When I was diagnosed with depression, the first person I called was my dad. I could finally understand what he dealt with for so many years, though his depression was never diagnosed.

Curtis K. Lawson (Sacramento, CA)

I remember talking to my uncle when he came home – not from prison but a mental health facility in Savanah, GA. Everybody in our family called him crazy.

I realized through his journey the importance of mental health and self-care.

Raymond Frazier (Savannah, GA)

I am a twenty-six year father of three. My dad and I have a therapy session twice a month. So many things happened when I was growing up. Dad and I both realized that we were depressed so we sought help.

Brandon Abrams (New Haven, Connecticut)

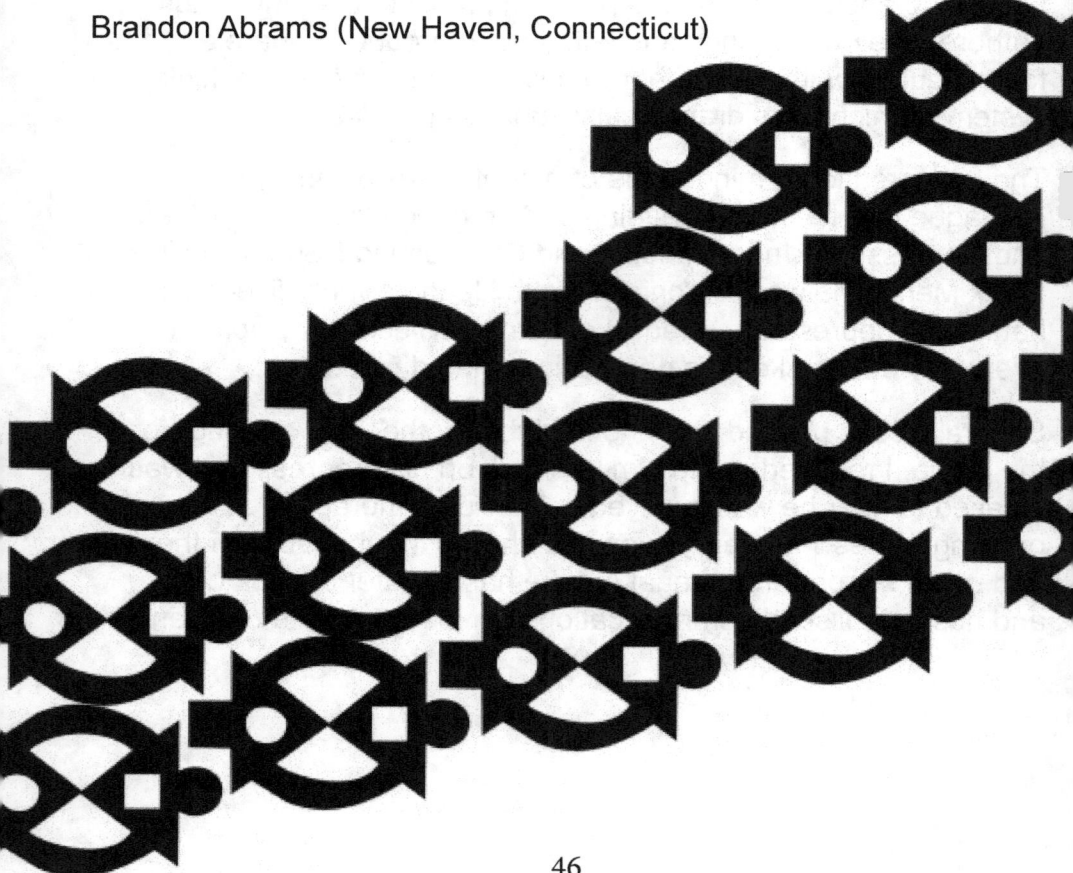

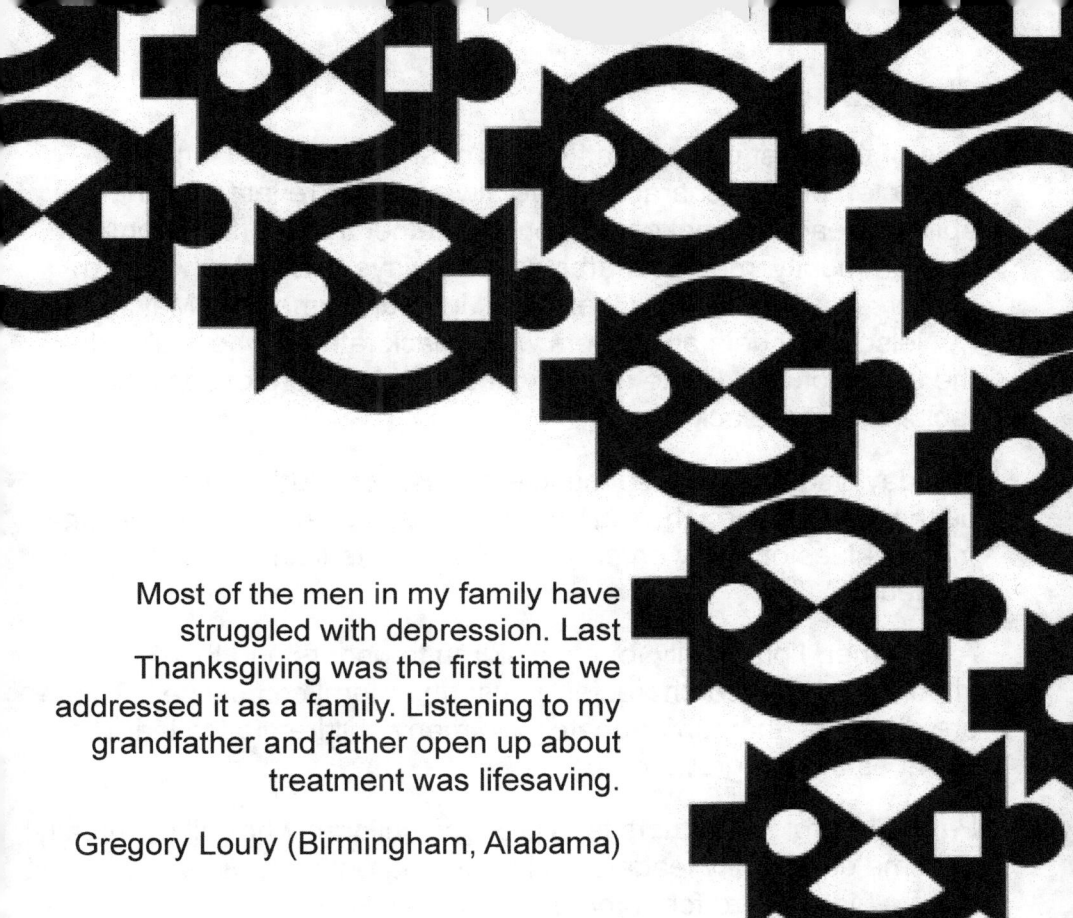

Most of the men in my family have struggled with depression. Last Thanksgiving was the first time we addressed it as a family. Listening to my grandfather and father open up about treatment was lifesaving.

Gregory Loury (Birmingham, Alabama)

I have been a therapist for the past ten years, practicing in Memphis, Tennessee. I became a therapist because years ago my dad suffered from major depression. Growing up, it was hard living with him, but we have gotten closer over the years. I learned from my dad's mental health challenges that Black men must focus greater attention on wellness.

Charles Ray (Fayetteville, NC)

Depression is a silent killer in the Black community. My father took his own life due to depression. It was a hard lesson for me to learn as a little boy

L.B. Washington (Portland, Oregon)

Character

One of the most powerful attributes of any successful father is character. Men of character have always been revered for their ability to lead and make decisions. Whether in the office, home or the community, men of character are always held in high regard. Fathers like Dr. Martin Luther King, Jr., Muhammad Ali, Malcolm X, Nelson Mandela and others were Black fathers who realized the power of virtues like honesty and integrity were essential for reclaiming the Black family.

In today's society, with so much emphasis on getting rich quick or becoming an overnight YouTube success, it seems the ethical and moral values of many entertainers and sports figures- have all but eroded.

As a father, I pray daily for my children to understand the importance of good character and sound moral compasses. These are attributes that, unfortunately, so many children fail to learn about as they're growing up.

Part of our role as fathers is to produce children who will eventually become community leaders and strong parents, individuals who will have a high regard for community and family life.

Tips for Building Character:

Demonstrate appropriate behavior. Losing your temper or cutting someone off on the highway, for instance, doesn't teach your children how to handle difficult situations. If you want your children to grow up to be levelheaded adults, practice being a level-headed adult around them.

Be Transparent. Share your own childhood experiences, particularly if you were bullied as a child or if you bullied kids just so you could belong to a clique. All of us adults have done some things we're not necessarily proud of, things we'd really rather our children didn't know. However, it's more important for us to share those things with them and face a bit of embarrassment than to let them make the same mistakes we did –which nowadays can be fatal.

Find teachable moments. Everyday situations that allow your children to witness the power of appropriate decision-making and managing difficult situations. There are "teachable" moments happening left and right in this country, in our schools, on the streets and even in churches. Never miss an opportunity to "teach" your children something.

The true measure of a man lies in the true character

of the individual.

Tony Albright (South Boston, Virginia)

My father died when I was ten ... My uncles taught me that your "word" still means something within this society.

Raheem Davis (Charleston, South Carolina)

"I have taught my sons that people are measured based on how their treatment of others ...

If African-American men are going to be respected in this country, we must treat each other fairly. Honesty must mean something!"

Jelani Pope (New Haven, Connecticut)

My sons are young, four and six; however, I must teach them to have a high regard for morality.

Jeff Craig (Petersburg, Florida)

"I've got mine; you've got yours to get!"

Al Watson (Atlanta, Georgia) – Basketball Coach

Character is something that I learned watching my father do business. He taught us that you are always "measured" based on how you conduct yourself.

Taz Martin (York, Pennsylvania)

I never met my "real" father; however, my stepfather helped me realize that a part of being a man is based on two things-dependability and character.

Ronnie Bishop (Dayton, Ohio)

CHAPTER FOUR
Family Life and Community Development

Understanding the notion that Black fathers are an essential part of family life and community development

Now I'm his dad. I live for [my son]. I have a responsibility. It's a big responsibility.

DJ Khaled

Family Life and Community Development

Dine with a stranger but save your love for your family.

~Ethiopian proverb~

For decades, we have heard the grim statistics on Black families, beginning with the infamous Moynihan Report written three years before I was conceived. Also known as the The Negro Family: The Case for National Action, the report was written by American sociologist Daniel Patrick Moynihan and commissioned by President Lyndon B. Johnson, affectionately known as LBJ.

Although written over fifty years ago, the report outlines a host of challenges that impact Black families. From access to jobs to the ability to find decent grocery stores in their neighborhoods, Black families struggle to get their share of the "so-called" American dream.

Few books, documentaries or feature news stories highlight the millions of good Black fathers across the earth. In fact, if you based your opinion of black fathers on what you see on the local news or read in newspaper and magazine articles, you'd likely think there are none – or too few to mention. However, my travels across the U.S. have afforded me the opportunity to visit communities and interact with thousands of Black families each year, many of which are led by a good Black man/father.

I often tell people I wish they could see Black America through my eyes. That's because I've seen the beauty of a young father walking down Chambers Street or Stonegate Drive in Flint, Michigan, carrying his baby. I've borne witness to good men like my father, Peter Miller, who are married to their children's mother and are in the home daily teaching their kids what they need to know to survive, teaching their sons how to become men. I know there are millions of good Black fathers out there. I am one, as are many of my friends and colleagues.

Each year when Father's Day rolls around, men always joke about how easy it is to get restaurant reservations as opposed to on Mother Day when you may wait two hours to be seated and another hour or longer before your food arrives. Yet Father's Day is a perfect time to highlight the unique contributions fathers. However, why should this celebration be relegated only to a single day in June? Much of the data that has bantered around underscores the role fathers play in the lives of their children.

> I have been married for sixteen years. The first four years were difficult. We talked about divorce, but through counseling and family support, we weathered the storms.
>
> The challenges with my wife helped me understand the importance of reconnecting with my father. We were distant over the years, but we have become closer.
>
> Forgiveness is important!
>
> Kendall Jones (Sacramento, California)

Discussing unique stories of fathers – even those who never experienced daily love and affirmation from their own dads – is critical. Yet we live in a society that focuses much of its energy demonizing Black fathers and scrutinizing our ability to be effective parents.

Most Black fathers can remember the day their children were born. It's a day filled with excitement, stress, anxiety and uncertainty. But most of all, it's a day filled with love and the realization that our primary job is to affirm our children and to do everything we can to protect them in a world that has become quite toxic, particularly for children of color.

Love

Today's society can be characterized as a microwave society. In other words, people are conditioned to want things immediately. Whether it's a high-paying job, a new car or falling in love instantly, most of us want what we want right away. One of the most important, yet undervalued, human emotions is love.

Throughout time, love has repaired relationships, ended family disputes and helped parents get through hard times. Love always will be the universal emotion that we all seek regardless of color, class or demographics.

Fathers, and not just mothers, must practice unconditional love with their children. The love between a father and his children can be priceless! Likewise, a father's love can be expressed many ways, from the simplicity of helping his child complete a task for the first time to acknowledging pride by smiling when a kid brings home an "A" on a spelling test.

If the Black community is going to survive, we must bring love back into our homes. Love is the fundamental emotion that we simply must have if we are to reduce the likelihood that our children will wind up in jail, in recovery houses or in cemeteries!

Perhaps 1 Corinthians 13:13 says it best: Faith, hope and love abide these three. But the greatest of these is love.

> **Fathers who teach their children how to love will create a generation of males who accept women and recognize that violence against them is wrong!**

While spending four years in prison, I forgot how to love. When I was released, I had to relearn was love was all about. It took me a while to reconnect with my children.

After being home for two years, I now have a strong and loving relationship with my two youngest children.

I am still working on my relationship with my oldest daughter, who lives on the West Coast. My father taught me that relationships take work. I took his advice.

Bilal Monroe (Mobile, Alabama)

I never knew my biological father. My mom helped me learn some important lessons about being a man. My basketball coach (Mr. Rice) entered my life during my freshman year and gave me the playbook on how to be a man and a great student-athlete.

Craig Witherspoon, Jr.
(Boston, Massachusetts)

I never met my father. My grandfather was the only father I ever knew. He died a few years ago, but he taught me how to be a great father and husband.

Kyle Henderson
(Newark, New Jersey)

We use the word love a lot, but I can truly say that my father loved me unconditionally.

Kevin Nelson
(Omaha, Nebraska)

You can't say you love yourself
if you do not take care of your children.

Malik Valentine (East Lansing, Michigan)

"
The love of a sober, responsible father can be the single greatest asset in the life of a boy. "

Lou Gathers (Cleveland, Ohio)

I love my sons more than life itself.
I am willing to die for my children.

Steve O'Neal (Pine Bluff, Arkansas)

A father's love and guidance can help boys navigate within the society.

Glen Moses (Long Island, New York)

Although I have never met my father, my grandfather helped me realize that love is more powerful than hate.

I used to hate my father for leaving ...

I have learned to love him through the love of my grandfather. I hope to meet him one day!

James Abraham (Toledo, Ohio)

Marriage

Historically, marriage has served as the foundation for community life and family development. Fathers serve as the model to help boys understand the significance of marriage and its role within society. In today's society, with the devastation that Black families have endured, marriage and the construction of healthy male/female relationships are critical to breaking the cycle of nonfunctioning families.

I remember reading an article almost a decade ago about a journalist interviewing Black children in Washington, D.C. about the concept of marriage. During the interview, several of the teens were amazed by the conversation and shared that they thought marriage was for white people only.

> My parents were never married. I never saw my dad in a stable relationship. To be honest, he was a player most of his life.
>
> Even so, he would always try to give me advice about women and relationships. I learned more from my football coach about relationships than I did from my dad. Mr. Akers was a great father and husband. We started every practice with prayer, and he made sure his players honored and respected women.
>
> Kareem Taylor (Flint, Michigan)

Having been raised by two loving parents who were married for over fifty years, the ideal of marriage is sacred to me. Seeing my parents endure the good and bad times made me a better man and eventually a better father.

Fathers must be in place to promote marriage and family planning, critical lessons that they should be required to teach and model for their families... The institution of marriage must be "held up" as meaningful within the Black community.

If we want our children to have successful marriages, we must ensure that they learn how to manage relationships and master communication at a young age.

If you think you want to marry a woman, sit down and talk. Talk about everything. You have got to agree on almost everything. If you can't agree, don't get married. My wife and I talked. I told her, 'If you don't hit me, I won't hit you.' We never had any trouble.

Vincent KilPatrick (Jacksonville, FL)

If "Black men" are going to get married, they must learn early the value of women. This is the lesson that all the men in my family learn."

Terry Neale (Akron, Ohio)

I learned how important marriage was by watching my father. My mom and stepdad were married thirty-three years. I never saw them disrespect each other.

Jermaine Wilkes (Birmingham, Alabama)

Fathers set the stage for boys to be marriage eligible. We must do a better job of encouraging our sons to marry women of African descent.

Malcolm Jenkins (Atlanta, Georgia)

My wife helped to "save me from myself." As I have gotten older, I have learned some valuable lessons about manhood and fatherhood.

Javier Smith
(San Diego, California)

Marriage is a key benchmark for manhood. At some point, every man should get married as part of the cycle of manhood.

Omar Frazier
(Dallas, TX)

SEX

Perhaps sex is one of the most important conversations a father can have with his son. This vital conversation must occur early and often. As our children become sexually active at an early age, fathers must be emotionally prepared to have conversations with their sons and daughters as early as eight years of age. We have all heard horror stories of elementary school aged children involved in sex acts in schools. Please understand while this may sound ridiculous, it's a true statement. Kids are growing up way too fast nowadays, and parents can't be stuck in the "old days" when parents virtually NEVER talked to their children about sex, no matter how old they were.

Fathers play a key role in teaching their sons about "male pregnancy" prevention and other aspects of male responsibility. Men have a moral and ethical responsibility to encourage boys to delay sex until they are emotionally able to handle the potential repercussions – like STDs or fatherhood.

Fathers can help their daughters understand key lessons about relationships and how younger males view sex and dating. Fathers should also be the first man to take their daughters on a date or to open car doors for them. Fathers should teach their daughters how they should expect – and get – respect from the men in their lives.

As long as we allow BET, MTV and local radio stations to frame the "discussion" around sexuality, we will continue to raise generations of children who will be involved in sex way to early.

My stance might not be a popular one, but let us take a moment to think about the alarming amounts of garbage that children digest on a regular basis. From "Love & Hip Hop" to the numerous music videos that promote sex daily, several programs on BET aren't necessarily appropriate for our children to watch. Our children should be able to come to us to learn about something as important as sex, and our relationship with our children should be such that they should know they can come to us.

Sex is a young man's biggest vice. Learn how to use your "big head" to control your "little head."

Melvin Travis
(Denver, Colorado)

My father did a good job of helping me understand sex and its power. Sex is not something for young men to take lightly!

Marquis Armstrong
(Oakland, California)

I remember my father's early letters from prison. Although he was away, he gave me solid advice about women and sex.

He would say, you have the ability to control your own destiny. Don't let your need for sex put you in situations that you won't be able to get out of.

Gus Gray
(Macon, Georgia)

Because my father was in my life, I avoided having sex before I was ready. So many of friends got girls pregnant while we were in high school.

Carlos
(Atlanta, Georgia)

As fathers, we must educate our daughters about the power of sex.

Our daughters will rely on television to get information about sex – or boys who will say everything they want to hear just to get what they want – if fathers are not present!

Fred Jefferson
(Winston-Salem, North Carolina)

Money

Next to sex, money is one of the most important areas that we fail to discuss with our children. Additionally, the lack of financial planning in households leads to martial challenges and, in many cases, divorce. Most successful marriages recognize that financial planning and transparency about money are key for a healthy marriage.

Everywhere you turn, a great deal of emphasis is placed on "getting paid." Society has become obsessed with getting rich, living in lavish homes and driving six-figure cars.

The power of money and the ability to use money as a tool to open doors are among the key lessons that fathers must position themselves to teach their children. This requires that fathers themselves are practicing financial responsibility.

> Fathers have an obligation to increase their children's awareness of business and commerce as basic elements of family and community life. Within the Black community, so many young people are sadly and mistakenly convinced that money is the key to happiness and pursuing happiness requires selling their souls or compromising their values.
>
> Often, the lack of business ownership doesn't allow the community to reinvest in itself. Thus, it becomes difficult to become self-sufficient and control finances without ownership!

My father taught my brothers, sisters and me about the accumulation and management of money ... Have a plan of action for life and be flexible and disciplined to ensure that you are reaching your goals.

Omar Khadir
(Bowie, Maryland)

During my first marriage, we never discussed money. My first marriage lasted two years. Money and the lack of communication around money destroyed our relationship. My parents never talked to us about money while we were growing up. I remember hearing my parents have heated arguments about money.

Ray Peterson
(Washington, DC)

My father grew up in the Nation of Islam. He taught all of us the importance of business ownership. Because of my father's influence, I am a serial entrepreneur.

David Muhammad
(Detroit, Michigan)

Always use money as a tool to leverage other resources. Money should be used to make more money.

Will Butler
(Houston, Texas)

My father told me "it's hard to be free if you do not own anything." My father stressed the importance of business development and ownership ... I created a business several years ago to be able to employ my son when he gets older.

Kevin Watson
(Silver Spring, Maryland)

My parents instilled in us a sense of money and business at an early age. I have always wanted to follow in my father's footsteps to be a business owner.

Solomon Johnston
(Chicago, Illinois)

Anytime the police can beat a "Black male" and it is captured on television, we need to realize that justice exists only for some.

Leon Garner
(Brooklyn, New York)

My father always warned me about the courts and the police.

Although they are supposed to serve and protect us all, if you are not "white," these assumptions don't always apply.

Eduard Riveria
(San Antonio, Texas)

Justice

When we talk about justice and the Black community, we get emotional very quickly. Why? Because of the countless times we've seen video footage of Black people being assaulted or outright murdered by police. Even when these murders are captured on film, and even when the victims are unarmed and posing no real threat to the cops, more often than not the courts are unable to render guilty verdicts against the officers.

The murders of Stephon Clark, Oscar Grant, Trayvon Martin, Tamir Rice, Freddie Gray, Jordan Davis and Michael Brown raise serious questions for fathers about safety and the role fathers must play in protecting the family.

If we want justice, we must develop an "insult level" that creates greater levels of activism within the community. This level of activism must begin with fathers setting standards and expectations for change within the community. If men are always absent, the challenges of injustice will not change – or they will change much more slowly than we need them to change.

Fathers are responsible for teaching and helping our children cope with the inequalities that exist within society. Fathers have an obligation to teach boys how to interact with the police and other entities that many cause them harm! They have an obligation to teach their daughters, too. (Need I remind you of Sandra Bland?) However, it seems cops tend to physically abuse and murder our Black men at much higher rates than they do our Black women.

It was hard for me to explain the death of Stephon Clark to my ten-year-old. I had to figure out the language to help him understand the seriousness of police stops.

Howard Smith
(Columbia, South Carolina)

Don't ever expect any justice from this society. Most people in this country have never seen us (American Indians) except for on television. Injustice has been how our land has been stolen and destroyed.

Jim Joseph (Tuscan, Arizona)

The best thing my father ever told me was to demand justice even if I didn't think I would get it. Justice and equality are worth fighting for.

Keith Vance (Newark, New Jersey)

" I remember growing up in Mississippi, where getting pulled over by the police became a regular routine for "Black Men" I learned how to deal with the police by watching my father

(because) he was always calm and cool.

"He knew that the police would kill him."

T.J. Jackson
(Savannah, Georgia)

"

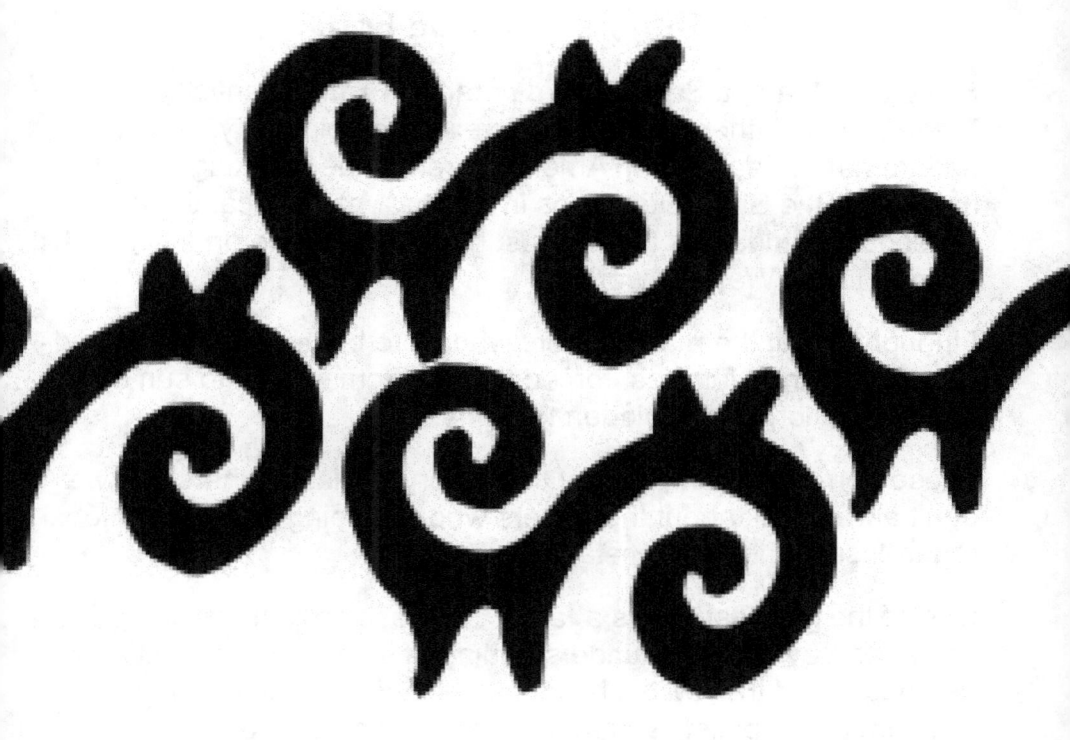

CHAPTER FIVE
Fathers as a God Force

Belief that Black fathers play a critical role in healthy child development and maturation

No need to fix what God already put his paintbrush on
- J. Cole

Fathers as a God Force

Since the Maafa, a Swahili word meaning "Transatlantic Slave Trade", Black fathers have always relied on spirituality as a tool to endure harsh treatment in America. I remember thinking on one of my trips to the Slave Dungeons in Ghana, West Africa, the kind of intestinal fortitude and faith it must have taken to be on a slave ship headed to the Western world.

I thought about the many fathers who were beaten, degraded and ripped from their families, forced to work from sun up to sun down on a plantation and forbidden to marry.

Those horrors are only part of the history of black fathers, yet we don't always talk about the fathers who are doing exceptional jobs regardless of their circumstance.

One of the greatest things a father can pass on to his children is the power of prayer and an understanding of spirituality. When times get tough, and they will, a belief in something greater than yourself is an important belief system for our children to have.

Below are few tips to help fathers:

Develop a ritual of prayer (consistent prayer and quiet time are essential)	**Give back** (practicing empathy and volunteering help the soul)
Reflect daily on your beliefs (write down that which you hold true. Discuss your beliefs with your children, family and friends)	**Study your faith** (become an expert in your faith's tradition)

Spirituality and yoga were two important things I learned from my dad to help me thrive in the toxicity of America.

Omar Wilson
(St. Louis, Missouri)

I remember going to church with my parents as a child. My dad was really involved at the church and taught us the importance of religion and spirituality.

I'm now a father of six, and I understand the importance of teaching my children about GOD and spirituality – thanks to the valuable lessons I learned from my father.

Kevin Mitchell (Omaha, Nebraska)

We grew up in the Deep South, and God and church were staples in our household. Every morning before school, we prayed as a family before we left the house.

I learned how to pray by watching my dad.

Curtis Jacobs (Natchez, Mississippi)

Raised by a Baptist preacher, we were at church every Sunday and many other days during the week. Learning how to pray and believing in a God force has always been part of life.

My father exposed us to the power of spirituality early in life.

Ed J. Thomas (Philadelphia, Pennsylvania)

Growing in my house, you had to go church. Even when I came home from college, I had to get up for church, even if I got home at three a.m. from the club.

Sean Jackson (Richmond, Virginia)

Prayer is part of my daily ritual. It was part of my father's daily ritual and his father's daily ritual!

Donte Johnson (Dallas, Texas)

Empathy

Two of the most profound lessons I learned from my father were empathy and the importance of giving back. These two traits are part of my daily life. Whether it's hosting community service projects or spending a few minutes daily talking to homeless men and women, caring about other people is an important trait that I've passed on to my children.

It amazes me how selfish we have become as a society. People seem to be too busy on their cell phones to notice human suffering. While most school districts promote service-learning hours, as fathers we must ensure that our children understand empathy and the importance of giving back to the less fortunate.

Teach your children how to serve others-- Find opportunities to volunteer

Talk to your children about kindness-- Help them understand that you treat people the way you would like to be treated.

Donate clothes and toys-- Encourage your children to give away clothes and toys each year to charities, and not just at Christmas time. Sure, children love toys at Christmas, but some children wouldn't get toys on their birthdays if it weren't for the kindness of others.

Help elderly neighbors—It's a great way to connect to the elders oEvery year we would donate clothes to a shelter in Denver. My father was big on giving back. This has become an annual ritual with my children.

Every year my family selects a charity to support. I adopted this practice from my father.

Michael Butler
(Norfolk, Virginia)

During the holiday months, we adopted a family in the housing projects where my dad and his family lived.

My dad created this tradition shortly before he passed away five years ago.

Calvin Williams
(Chicago, Illinois)

Having been homeless in the past, I know that giving back is important.

I can still remember my grandfather would always take us to deliver dinners to homeless shelters in Washington, DC.

Frank Carter
(Washington, DC)

CHAPTER SIX
Building Legacies

My favorite thing about being a father is just seeing my kids grow and do some of the same things that I did when I was a kid, man.

Lebron James-- Cleveland Cavaliers

Honoring and celebrating Black fathers should be viewed as an important function for preserving families

Manhood

In the world of boys, the quest for manhood can in many cases becomes a journey into the unknown.

Fathers are the first line of defense for boys trying to navigate the mazes of obstacles that confront their path to manhood. Fathers are responsible for the education, nurturing and, to some extent, the ideals young men associate with the construct of manhood.

This includes understanding, respecting and protecting women and girls. Too many girls and women are being abused at the hands of Black men and boys. This problem must be addressed and corrected to produce healthy notions of manhood and rebuild trust between Black men and women.

As many have pointed out over time, manhood is not something that occurs solely by a boy reaching his eighteenth birthday. Much preparation, support and encouragement are needed to ensure our boys will eventually become men in every sense of the word.

Our children deserve to go through a "rite of passage" that will help them understand the complexities of manhood and masculinity. This passage will serve as a blueprint for boys that will ultimately determine whether we can deter our sons from going to prison.

Without defined criteria for manhood, many seek answers in material things, popular trends and negative influences. For example, they think they have to have the latest Air Jordans, the phattest Timberland boots or the most expensive rims on the market, and some of them won't think twice about resulting to illegal activity to get those items. Likewise, I don't have to tell you that some of the Black men in prison are there, in part, because the only people who bothered to teach them about manhood were drug dealers who they began idolizing and following down some really bad paths.

Finally, the transition from boyhood to manhood must be taken seriously to raise healthy Black boys. We can no longer wait until our sons are teenagers to begin addressing issues related to manhood. Our sons need our unconditional love, attention and support to navigate the obstacles and pitfalls that often confront males of African descent.

I have raised four strong Black males. The key was helping my sons understand "what men do!" I taught them what I learned from the men in my family.

It wasn't easy, but at least I had a model of manhood to draw from.

Robert Gardner
(New Haven, Connecticut)

Raising three teen daughters has been the joy of life.

I was fortunate to be raised by a loving stepfather who guided me through manhood.

Larry Jennings
(Fayetteville, North Carolina)

Teaching my sons about manhood was essential for their survival. I learned so many life lessons from fathers figure as I was growing up.

Khalil Wright
(Knoxville, Tennessee)

The father and daughter relationship is incredibly important. I remember watching how my dad treated my sisters.

Now that I have daughters, I do exactly what my dad did!

Kofi Stewart
(Seattle, Washington)

Clearly understanding manhood helps boys navigate a society that often destroys Black male potential.

David Kendall
(Baltimore, Maryland)

I can't wait to become a father so I can teach my son the lessons I learned from my father about manhood.

Andre Dallas
(Brownsville, Texas)

A man who can't admit when he is wrong is a manwho will never be right. I would hear this from my grandfather all the time.

Keith Gerrod
(Columbia, Maryland)

Fathers set the tone for manhood in communities. When fathers are not present, issues around manhood will arise.

Greg Anderson
(Lancaster, Pennsylvania)

<u>Advice</u>

What does it mean to be a father? The art of fatherhood is evolving as society changes and the expectations and demands of fatherhood increase. Fathers need to help their children build confidence and self-esteem, and in turn, learn how to be engaged with, supportive of and loving r to their children.

One of the greatest roles fathers play is providing solid advice based on lessons they learned and experiences they had while growing up. We have all heard the phrase, "Your parents are your first teachers."

I remember asking my father questions on a variety of topics as I was growing up. Dad always took the time to answer my questions. And while I didn't always like the advice he imparted, as I got older I realize my father's insightful wisdom was based on mistakes he'd had already made and was hoping to prevent me from making.

Four important tips:

Spend time with your child. How a father spends his time reveals to his child what's important to him.

Be your childs role model. Whether they realize it or not, fathers are role models to their children.

Eat together as a family. An important part of healthy family life is bonding through family meals.

Earn the right to be heard. Fathers should begin having conversations with their children about important topics when they are very young so that difficult subjects will be easier to handle as they get older.

> " The best advice my father ever gave me was to take advice only from people who are happy. "
>
> Romell Thomas
> (Queens, New York)

The advice I have received from my father and father figures has been life changing. I have been blessed to have so many Black men in my life who provided constant wisdom and encouragement through my lifetime.

Tim Smith
(Rockford, Illinois)

Advice will come from many people.
You have to judge what works for you.

Kato Wilson
(Philadelphia, Pennsylvania)

I had many father figures corning up. Each one gave me good advice that helped me become the father I am now.

Lenny Nelson
(Youngstown, Ohio)

As a young father, I hope I will be able to give my kids life-saving advice.

Al King
(Richmond, Virginia)

Fatherly advice as well as the "community of men" are essential to maintaining healthy community life. I have a great father who has always supported me.

Saul Smith
(Boston, Massachusetts)

I have raised my son and two stepsons. It is my hope that the advice I have given them will assist them throughout their journey towards manhood.

Bruce Bowling
(Dover, Delaware)

A father's advice can make the difference between our sons making a lifetime of bad decisions.

Clyde (Memphis, Tennessee)

Fatherhood is the most rewarding job that you will ever have. It will bring you rewards that far exceed money and power ...

Real power is raising your sons to have a better quality of life than you had.

Earle James (U.S. Virgin Islands)

I wish I had listened to the advice of my father. I didn't listen, and as a result, my son was sentenced to ten years in prison.

My son wanted to follow in my footsteps to become a drug dealer. My father warned me that boys ultimately want to be like their fathers (whether good or bad)

Yusef Muhammad (Norfolk, Virginia)

I teach my sons that men build communities, not tear them down! This was my father's daily mantra.

J.L. Brown (Minneapolis, Minnesota)

Honoring Our Mothers

Our mothers have been undervalued and marginalized since slavery. Fathers, regardless of the history and circumstances of the relationship, must honor the mothers of their children – even when the mothers have exhibited behaviors that don't require them to be respected.

The fact remains that single mothers have been demonized for too long. Mothers represent the foundation of community life and development. Thus, our sons need to see men respecting women. All too often, our sons see men disrespecting and degrading women. Unfortunately, our sons see this kind of behavior and begin to think it is acceptable.

Fathers must be willing to step up and become active partners in the raising of our boys. We have allowed too much time to pass and too many families to be affected by the phenomenon of the absent daddy club.

Mothers have been the "glue" keeping so many families intact. It is time for men to celebrate mothers and figure out ways to amicably work with them to raise our boys!

Honoring our mothers is important. Part of being a strong father is respecting the contributions of women. Throughout slavery and to the present, Black women have held the family together.

Dre Jackson (Jackson, Mississippi)

Helpful Tips:

Always respect your mom, even when it is difficult.

Set healthy boundaries.

Don't try to change your parents.

It is important to forgive your mom for things that may or may not have happened during your childhood

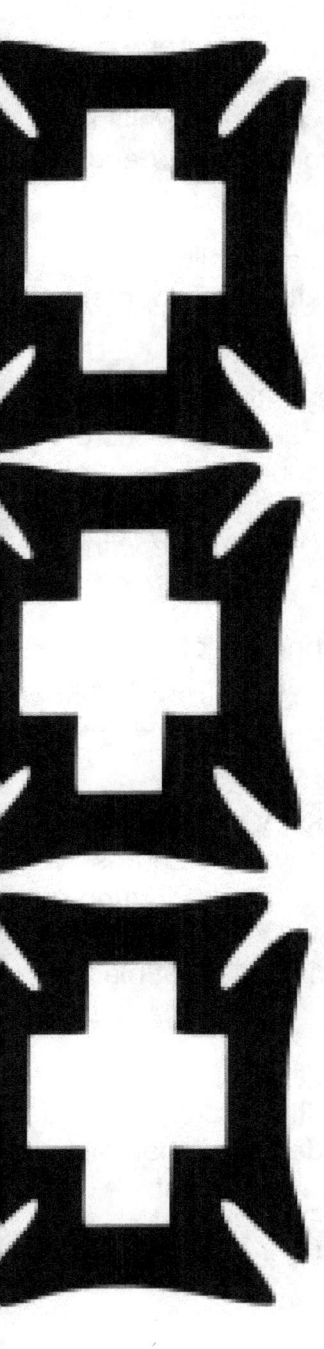

The advice I give to others that was given to me from my stepfather, who helped to raise me, is that we receive only one mother in our lifetime. No matter how mad we may be at our mother, for whatever reason, she is still our mother and the Most High will always expect us to demonstrate the love and respect we have for her.

Lawrence Knight
(Houston, Texas)

I didn't always like my mother because of the things she used to say about my father. Over time, my father has helped me realize that in life you get only one set of parents!

Gerrod Mayo
(Buffalo, New York)

Mothers are and have been the backbone of the Black community. We must teach our sons to respect the girls and women in the community. They will be or are already mothers!

Lucky Jones
(Detroit, Michigan)

As a father, even though I am not with my child's mother. I realize my son needs to see me interact positively with his mother!

Clive Charles, Jr.
(Baton Rouge, Louisiana)

Our mothers are the backbone of the community. Without our mothers, I'm not sure what our communities would look like.

Malachi Lindsey
(Birmingham, Alabama)

Raising Sons

Raising sons in a toxic society is no easy task. Raising boys can no longer be considered solely the responsibility of women. The pressures that confront Black male children are both numerous and complex. From navigating encounters with the police to walking through the neighborhood on the way home from school, dangers await our sons at every turn.

Today's Black father assumes an awesome responsibility of being a nurturer, protector and teacher to ensure healthy development of Black male children.

Realizing that often parents don't see eye to eye, the key to raising a son lies within the parent's ability to make the needs of the child the focal point. All too often, the emotional and spiritual development of the son takes a backseat to the parent's inability to be mature adults. As this becomes a reoccurring theme with so many parents, ultimately the male child suffers.

All too often, the emotional and spiritual development of the son takes a backseat to the parents' inability to be mature adults. As this becomes a reoccurring theme with so many parents, ultimately the male child suffers.

On countless occasions, I have been contacted by single moms from across the country whose anger, frustration and bitterness with "dad" stands in the way of healthy parenting practices. Figuring out strategies for men and women to work collectively is an important step toward ensuring the physical and emotional safety of black male children.

Fathers are responsible for creating the earliest foundation for boys to understand the world of men. Raising a healthy, productive male of African descent requires mentoring and modeling by men and women who are committed to family life and development.

If we really want to improve the life chances of our sons, we must begin to act, now!

In terms of raising my son, I absolutely have to raise his male friends as well. This was how my father ran things in my house. He helped mentor all of the young brothers in my crew.

Eric Bellamy
(Cleveland, Ohio)

My father helped me understand that we have to build men. It starts when they are boys. What lessons do they learn early?

J.T. Scott
(Columbia, South Carolina)

I learned so much from my father that will help me raise my boys. My father instilled in us a solid work ethic, notion of responsibility and a strong belief in family first. These are the things that boys need to be taught before they are seven-years-old

Gary Temple
(Dayton, Ohio)

My father taught me that no curriculum exists for raising boys. The key is very simple: love, respect and mutual respect for humanity.

John Mack
(Chapel Hill, North Carolina)

I learned from my stepfather (Joshua) that the deposit of time spent with your children may not be recognized until long after your ability to hear.

Kenneth Braswell
(Atlanta, Georgia)

Although I never knew my father, due to his absence I realized how important fathers are to raising healthy black boys. My single goal in life is to be the best father I can be!

Thomas Childs
(Rochester, New York)

The women in my family have always raised the children. I know that I must step up to raise my five sons.

Khalid Bishop
(Detroit, Michigan)

Making Mistakes

In life many lessons exist that help us along the way. Making mistakes and dealing with those mistakes are part of the life lessons that children eventually encounter. Making mistakes in life is normal and customary. However, the steps that we take to remedy the mistakes we make are crucial.

When children make mistakes, responsible fathers are needed to help them rationalize and implement strategies to deal with the repercussions. Fathers play a major role in teaching, coaching and modeling ways to deal with life's mistakes.

Fathers ultimately play a role in how our children problem-solve during difficult situations. The role of the father, although often minimized, can't and shouldn't be taken for granted!

Our children will make mistakes regarding girls, friends, etc. It is essential that fathers are in place to help children get vital information to reduce the number of life threatening" mistakes they will make in their lives.

Things fathers should discuss with their children to help them process the mistakes they make:

What did you learn from your decision?

What would you have done differently with additional information?

Always fix a problem, especially if you are responsible for it… correct your mistakes.

Bleek (Baltimore, Maryland)

The things my father taught me I have transmitted to my five sons. For every mistake you make, an opportunity exists to correct that mistake. Men own up to mistakes. We don't run from our mistakes.

Michael Daniels (Savannah, Georgia)

My father served as a "buffer" in my life. He helped me handle many of the challenges that young males face ... My father will always be a giant of a man. I hope that I can be half of the man that my father was to me and my children.

Matthew Edmond (Columbia, South Carolina)

Part of being a man is making mistakes. As a father who is raising two boys "alone," I need to be present to help my sons be a sounding board when they make mistakes.

Jameel Painter (Bronx, New York)

Mistakes becomes life's best teacher. At least you learn what not to do the next time!

Carl Williams (Syracuse, New York)

Friends

Growing up I would always hear the term «wrong place at the wrong time. Many times our children find themselves in trouble based on the company they keep. Selecting friends is a key development factor in the lives of children and parents.

Having a solid relationship with our children ultimately determines the information they will share with us about their daily lives. When fathers create a healthy balance between work and home, it enables them to spend more quality time with their children. Spending time listening to children share information about their school day and or other events that are important in their life is critical for fathers to do.

Spending quality time with their sons builds strong relationships and strengthens communication between fathers and their children. Fathers need to set a tone that encourages children to be prepared to make decisions about friendships and relationships!

The following are some basic questions that fathers must ask themselves:

Do you know your child's or children's friends? (Moreover, do you have their telephone numbers?)

Do you know or have you met the parents of your child's or children's friends?

Are you aware of the places your child or children and his/their friends frequent?

My father would always say to me: Choose your friends wisely or they may eventually become your enemies.

Warrick Chambers
(Pontiac, Michigan)

True friends correct you when you are wrong. Enemies don›t because they are building the foundation for your destruction.

Terry Avon
(Baltimore, Maryland)

Learning the role of friendship begins with the relationship between a father and son.

Alex Thomas
(Baton Rouge, Louisiana)

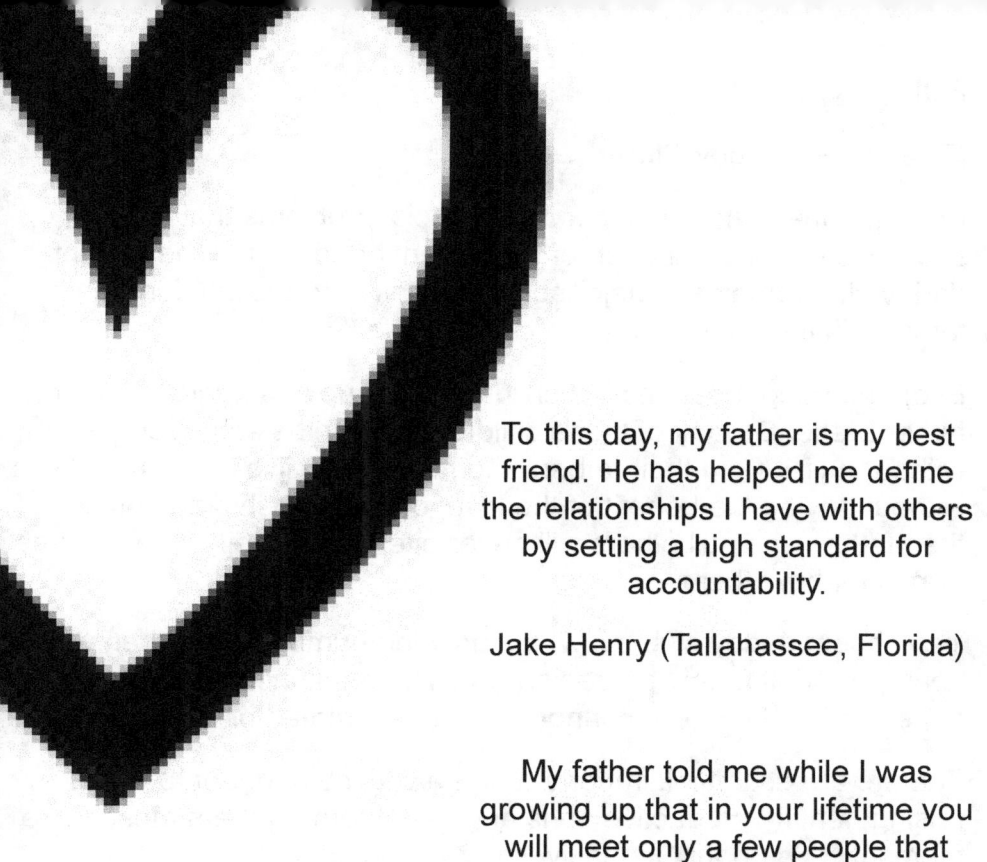

To this day, my father is my best friend. He has helped me define the relationships I have with others by setting a high standard for accountability.

Jake Henry (Tallahassee, Florida)

My father told me while I was growing up that in your lifetime you will meet only a few people that you can really call friends.

Mack Lewis (Toledo, Ohio)

Friends are like tires on a car. You will eventually have to get new ones. I would hear this from my basketball coach. This was the best advice I received from a father figure.

Tony Kendrick (Akron, Ohio)

Fatherless

(The Absent Daddy Club)

Perhaps one of the most pervasive social problems that affects society is the phenomenon of the absent daddy club. The absent daddy club remains a major source of pain and anxiety for many families in the community.

Every morning thousands of children wake up in a house without a father present. Many of these children go months and even years without a visit from their fathers. Some children live their entire lives without having the benefit of the love, companionship and advice of their father, and still others will never even know their fathers' name or much about them.

The absent daddy club spawns a growing number of children who yearn for adult male companionship. The relationship between a father and a child (ren) cannot be underestimated or minimized.

Fathers are essential, important and a vital component to raising healthy/productive sons and daughters. Fathers must make themselves a priority in the lives of their sons!

If we are serious about improving the life chances of our children, fatherlessness and the role of fathers needs greater attention. We must begin to create and implement corrective measures that will reduce the likelihood that our children will become part of the absent daddy club. We can't afford to act as if this problem will simply go away. The issue of eliminating fatherlessness must be a priority if we are going to break the vicious cycle of Black children growing up without their dads. Just like a lot of children who grow up in abusive homes become abusers, a lot of children who grow up without their fathers end up being absent in their own children's lives.

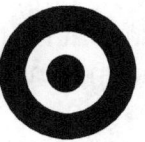

I went to prison angry at my father for leaving when I was twelve-years-old. I blamed everybody buy myself for the way my life turned out. I reconnected with my dad last year.

It's the best move I have made in my life.

Eugene Malone
(Stone Mountain, Georgia)

Needed my father when I was younger.

If he would have been around,
I may not have joined the "Crips."

As a father, I realized nothing
would keep me from my children.

Calvin Winters
(Los Angeles, California)

Having grown up without my father, I had to discover compassion and forgive him. Not for him, but for me. I nursed, nurtured and carried my anger through many years of depression ... I am now at a better place by realizing that as painful as my father's absence was, I've become stronger, more informed and wiser about fatherhood.

Martin Glynn (United Kingdom)

As I look back on my life, as a young man growing up in inner-city (Washington, D.C) one of three boys being raised by a single mother, I highlight as significant the fact that my mother never had anything negative to say about my father ... Despite the situation, I can say today that I love my father, and my love for him has made me a better person.

Mike Caldwell (Washington, D.C.)

Give our sons a strong identity and foundation. The rest will fall in place.

Peter (Troy, California)

I really believe in my heart of hearts that if my father were present when I was a teenager, I never would have gone to prison.

Devin Davenport
(Columbus, Ohio)

I learned the hard way that having a father could make the difference in the life of a boy. I just turned forty years of age, but I still miss my father.

Quentin Richardson
(Providence, Rhode Island)

More than anything else in life, I wish my father could be a grandfather to my sons.

Victor Jenkins
(Wichita, Kansas)

I met my father for the first time three years ago.

Our reunion has been painful, but it has helped me understand the power that fathers have in the lives of their sons.

Jamone Swinton
(Camden, New Jersey)

Work Ethic

Many attributes are required to ensure that our sons grow into healthy and productive contributors to society. Instilling a strong work ethic and forming solid notions about the meaning of hard work are key areas of development for young males.

I am often amazed at the numbers of men (fathers) who have not worked a legal job. It is difficult to teach our sons to have a "work ethic" if they don't see us working. The apple usually doesn't fall far the tree!

In today›s society, many of our children are allowed to skip school, smoke weed, play video games and participate in other activities. Work and the ability to earn an income are key components of becoming a man. These are lessons that fathers must be required to teach our sons. Boys that grow up without a solid work ethic often lack a major trait that boys desperately need.

Fathers that teach, coach and model the importance of work raise boys who will be successful and industrious!

Tips for fathers to teach children about developing a strong work ethic:

Create a list of chores--Start early having your children complete chores around the house.

Treat school like a job--If your kids are in school and bring home homework, teach them to treat school like a job and to do their homework as if a paycheck depended on it.

If you hire out, do a full day's work. I never understood that as a young man, but as an adult, I now do. What it means to me now is to be the best that I can be, at whatever I do.

Jim Boston
(Detroit, Michigan)

My father taught me very early in life that a man is measured by his work ethic.

Craig Rogers
(East Orange, New Jersey)

African-American fathers must teach their sons that work is the foundation of community life and development. This is one of the earliest lessons I learned from my father and other men in my family.

Gray Grandison (Long Beach, California)

The notion of work among African-American males is essential. Fathers are the primary mechanism for getting these lessons to their sons.

Miles Benjamin (Arlington, Virginia)

Work is something that men do. Having a strong work ethic is part of being a man. Males of African descent do not have time to be lazy ...Real men do not have time to play games.

Rome Thomas (Charleston, South Carolina)

Men and boys will always be judged based on two things: how they treat their mothers and whether or not they are involved in hard work.

Jay Owens (St. Louis, Missouri)

Life

Life and the quality of life are often discussion items among fathers and their children at kitchen tables throughout this country and abroad.

Fathers, in many respects, help our children craft a blueprint for how to be committed, responsible fathers in the lives of their children and for how to navigate through the obstacles and pitfalls that are present in society.

At the end of the day, fathers must be more involved in their children's lives. We have all witnessed the psychological effect and trauma that absent fathers inflict on their children. I'm always reminded of several youth I've worked with whose anger and rage were present over just the mention of the word father. The anger, resentment and bitterness are real and cause self-destructive behaviors among children.

This relationship must focus on fathers spending quality time with their children, versus making excuses because of child support payments and other issues related to money!

The following are some basic questions that we must ask our sons early and often:

What do you want out of life?

What steps must you take to achieve success?

Are you working on the skills you need to be successful?

You don't have to win every race you run.
I always appreciated my father giving me permission to fail and, by extension, permission to try again.

Orlando Peters (Los Angeles, California)

I always had the fear that I would die young, like him, but I am now forty-one … It is a profound and forever silence. In that silence, he lives – in me. His absence has taught me to listen and taught me to master the lesson in/of silence.

Devin Lawrence (Los Angles, California)

Don't be afraid to embrace change … It is the very ingredient that promotes growth.

Sam Johnson (Jersey City, New Jersey)

I am a problem solver. I relish confrontation as one aspect of negotiation. I take risks.

Al Wilson (Minneapolis, Minnesota)

Only two things show you a lot of teeth – sharks and wolves – and both of them are getting ready to kill you when you see them.

Alan Nelson (Baltimore, Maryland)

Death
====

Death is perhaps one of the most difficult subjects to discuss with children. The loss of a family member or friend can be traumatic experience for youth. Often, the children haven't developed the emotional equipment to deal with a sudden loss.

In urban communities, the sense of loss among males of African descent has reached epidemic proportions. The probabilities of males of African descent being engaged in violence increase the likelihood that homicide will remain a major cause of death among males of African descent.

According to the Centers for Disease Control (CDC), homicide remains the leading cause of death for males of African descent ages fifteen to twenty-four. With cities like Baltimore, Chicago, Detroit and Los Angeles recording large numbers of homicides among males of African descent, greater efforts are needed to teach, coach and mode lifestyles that promote alternatives to violence.

Fathers in the lives of youth can and will reduce homicide among males, Research strongly shows the relationship between parent involvement and success in young males.

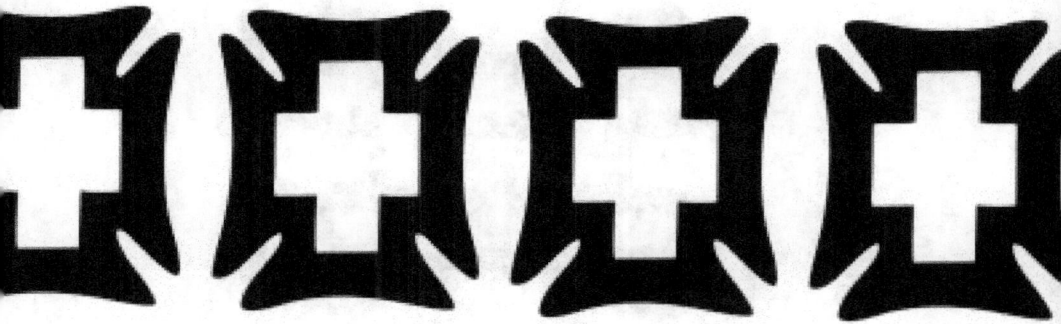

My father (off duty police officer) was killed while responding to a drug bust in Harlem, New York.

As a nine-year-old male without a father, I had to make a decision to become a Black man of purpose, education and character.

With fifteen years of continuous sobriety from drugs and alcohol, my pledge is to assist with the war on the destruction of young black men in our nation's cities.

Kevin Powers
(Phoenix, Arizona)

My father and grandfather always told me that if you are "living right," death becomes only an extension to your life.

Jean Thompson
(Macon, Georgia)

I want my son who is sixteen-years-old, to outlive me ... I "should" die before he does. However, among my son's friends, their parents outlive them. It is my responsibility to break the cycle. It starts with me as a father.

Jermaine Hughes
(Los Angeles, California)

Black males + bad decisions = Death. Our sons are confronted with this equation.

Steve Samson
(Richmond, Virginia)

My sons are trapped in a world that suggests that violence and drug dealing are acceptable lifestyles. I am afraid that they are going to die! I need to step up my game to help save their lives!

Miles Farmer
(Augusta, Georgia)

The Fatherhood Imperative

If we gave you a sheet of paper and a pencil and asked you to define the term "family," what would you write? The notion that there›s one definition of family is changing. Over the past twenty-five years, families have become more diverse. There are stay-at-home dads, two-parent as well as single-parent families, blended families, married as well as unmarried, cohabiting parents, heterosexual as well as same-sex parents, single-race as well as interracial families and two- as well as three-generational families.

These multiple configurations of families create a great deal of conversation around defining the roles of families. With all this being said, most people would still describe a family using terms like a unit, a group that lives together and works together. Others might be able to drill down and come up with a few concrete goals for a family.

While spend much time talking about the importance of families, we decided that it is critically important to provide fathers with a clearer understanding of the importance of family.

Unfortunately, society has changed over the last few decades. Many still underestimate the role of fathers in families. Most believe that fathers play a critical role in the development of their children; however, many fathers remain uncertain about the responsibilities and privileges associated with this role. This in part can be attributed to the changing landscape of values and believes.

With alarming rates of pregnancies to unwed mothers, skyrocketing divorce rates and the declining significance of fidelity, U.S. families struggle to raise healthy families.

As fathers, we felt that this is an area that needs greater exploration and guidance. Call us traditional, but we still believe that fathers are the backbone of families. We still understand that strong families need strong fathers that are willing to go the extra mile for the health, security and vitality of the family.

To this end, I have identified four core areas that fathers must focus on and develop short and long-term action plans to sustain. While these four areas are key, they are in no way the sole responsibility of fathers.

However, we believe that a focus on these areas sets a standard for the role of fathers in families:

- Spending quality time with the family
- Emotional and spiritual connection with his family
- Ensuring the family's financial survival
- Presenting an image of responsibility and a serious work ethic
- Giving back to the larger community
- Consistently encouraging other fathers
- Honoring, respecting and protecting Black women and girls

Being a Revolutionary Father Means:

- Realizing that spirituality and sobriety are essential ingredients for men who are interested in raising healthy children.

- Being nurturing and compassionate and teaching, coaching and modeling the essence of community and family life.

- Placing high value on integrity and morality.

- Viewing fatherhood as a critical component to improving the quality of life for children.

- Fostering emotional development among his children and teaching his children to have an emotional vocabulary.

- Demonstrating and coaching the importance of economic security and self-sufficiency. "Do for self and kind."

- Understanding that women are the mothers of creation and thus must be honored and respected.

- Maintaining «tactical anger" that motivates fathers to focus on family life and the preservation of the children.

- Being dogmatic and uncompromising when it pertains to the health, safety and emotional stability of his children.

- Creating an economic, political and spiritual blueprint for the family.

- Mastering the art of communication and language; Using communication as a tool to effectively navigate in society.

- Seeking counsel and advice from elders who promote family development.

- Expressing love and admiration for children and family, which are gifts from the Creator.

- Realizing that the emotional and physical protections of the family are keys to survival of the "clan".

- Honoring commitments and obligations, above all else!

When we get to the point of building boys who will become Revolutionary Fathers, we will create a safer world for our families!

Mental Health Alert

Do fathers ask for help?

Several years ago while facilitating an Intergenerational Men's Group in New Orleans, I and some of the other brothers met Nate, an investment banker with an MBA from the prestigious Wharton School from University of Pennsylvania. Nate decided to visit the group due to some challenges he was having with his wife.

Within the group, Nate shared that he was no longer spending quality time with his wife and two children. Nate was dealing with multiple issues:

1. Losing his grandparents during Hurricane Katrina;
2. Having lost his job several months ago and
3. Losing interest in being married.

Nate, like so many fathers, struggled with a "silent killer" in this nation.

The "silent killer" that is seldom discussed by men impacts millions, deals with the inability to manage emerging pressures stemming from societal changes, dynamics at work and in the family.

According to the National Institute of Mental Health, researchers estimate that at least six million men suffer from depression each year in the United States.

Nate, like many dads, could acknowledge his recent physical challenges — fatigue, headaches, irritability, loss of interest in work, lowered sexual drive and sleep disturbances — but Nate was unable to identify and acknowledge his emotional feelings of sadness, worthlessness, hopelessness and excessive guilt.

Nate's behavior became increasingly erratic with an increase of drinking and smoking marijuana. At the end of the group, several guys shared with Nate the power of therapy in their lives. As a result, Nate inquired about seeing a licensed professional.

Selecting a therapist can be a difficult process. It will take some time to get referrals from family and friends, as well as doing independent research on therapists in your area.

The following are a few helpful tips:

- Check the therapist's credentials (contact state licensing boards)
- Arrange time to meet with therapist
- Select a therapist with specific credentials and experience that address your core needs (For example, anger, abuse, and ADHD, etc. - Theory of practice/length of experience)
- Determine whether the therapist accepts insurance, offers a sliding scale fee and/or works pro bono? (Those are important questions to ask although many providers do take insurance)
- Find out whether the practice has any openings? If the answer is no, ask them to recommend a local therapist with similar experience
- How much does a typical hour-long session cost?
- What are the practice's hours and does it offer weekend sessions?

Below are a few organizations that can help you with your search:

National Association of Black Social Workers: www.nabsw.org

National Alliance of Mental Illness: www.nami.org

4 Things to consider

1. Reduce Stress

Rough day at work? Take a walk or head to the gym for a quick workout. One of the most common mental benefits of exercise is stress relief.

2. Seek professional help.

Finding a licensed professional can lead to a major breakthrough in your life. Take your time selecting a therapist with whom you can connect.

3. Name your pain

Whether it is related to something that occurred when you were a child or an adult, it's time to acknowledge your pain. It's impossible to begin healing without confronting your source of pain.

4. Help Control Addiction

We all have addictions, which can range from sex to gambling to video games to watching TV to shopping to food and, of course, to drugs and alcohol. Are your addictions affecting your ability to be a good, effective and loving father?

Homework Assignment

To My Children

Draft a letter to your children. Reflect on the values and virtues that you tried to instill in them. What characteristics do you see in your children?

___

___

___

___

___

___

___

Homework Assignment

Personal Declaration

Being a Black father in America can be difficult. Are you up for the challenge?

Take a few minutes and write down a list of prayers and affirmations that will continue to help you during your fatherhood journey.

_____

_____

_____

_____

_____

_____

_____

Adinkra Symbols

Throughout the book Adinkra symbols are used on several pages. Adinkra symbols are visual symbols, originally created by the Akan of Ghana and the Gyaman of Cote d'Ivoire in West Africa. Each Adinkra symbol represents traditional wisdom, affirm life and promote healthy mental, physical & spiritual life.

About The Author

David Miller is a father, husband and advocate for strengthening Black families. He is the founder of the Dare To Be King Project, a curriculum/training program designed to teach Black male youth how to survive and thrive in the toxicity of America. David has a master's degree in education from Goucher College and a bachelor's degree in political science from the University of Baltimore. Learn more about David and his work at www.daretobeking.net.

For speaking engagements, book signings and other information on our work with fathers and youth, please visit www.daretobeking.net.